Tiny Toes Adventures Australia

Rafiel Aharoni

Published in Saint Petersburg, FL

Printed in United States

Library of Congress Control Number: [2023916777]

ISBN:

Paperback [979-8-9889547-3-6]

In Sydney, little traveler, so much to see,
With the Opera House sails, as white as can be.
The Harbour Bridge arches, so grand and so high,
Seagulls whirl and twirl, up in the sky.
Ferries dance on the water, a shimmering blue,
Koalas and kangaroos wait just for you.
So, baby on board, with wonders anew,
Sydney's adventures are calling to you!

In Melbourne's embrace, baby, you'll find,
Skyscrapers tall and trams aligned.
Eureka Tower, shining so bright,
Yarra River gleaming in daylight.
Koalas hug and kangaroos hop,
In this Aussie city, the fun won't stop.
Cafés buzz and the footy's a cheer,
For a traveling baby, there's much to revere.
So gaze wide-eyed, take in the view,
Melbourne's wonders await you!

In Canberra, by the lake's soft sway,
Swans glide by, adding charm to your day.
Gaze at Telstra, so tall and fine,
With each new sight, you'll feel divine.
Parliament's doors, open and wide,
Where leaders and history reside.
Around every corner, tales unfurl,
For you, the traveling baby, to whirl!

In Brisbane's bright glow, you'll see,
The Wheel spinning high and free.
Gold Coast's waves, soft and grand,
Will tickle your tiny toes in the sand.
Koala hugs, beaches wide,
Exciting adventures on every side.
For a baby traveler, just like you,
Queensland's wonders will feel brand new!

In Cairns, baby, you'll find delight,
Where the sun shines oh-so bright.
Palm trees sway and beaches gleam,
Tropical wonders, like a dream.

Kangaroos hop, while koalas climb,
Birds sing their ancient, rhythmic rhyme.
The Great Barrier Reef's just a dive away,
With colors and fishes in vast array.

Tiny toes in warm, soft sand,
Discovering wonders, isn't it grand?
For a traveling baby, Cairns is a gem,
A place of wonder, just for them!

To Darwin's shores, young traveler, you glide,
Where golden sands kiss the azure tide.
Kangaroos hop, and palm trees sway,
Underneath the sun's warm array.
Tiny toes in soft sand delve,
Discovering wonders all by yourself.
The Timor Sea's gentle hum,
Welcomes you with its salty strum.
With each new sight and sound so neat,
Baby's journey is truly sweet!

To Uluru, baby, you'll glide,
Where ancient rocks reside.
Red sands beneath your tiny toes,
The heart of Australia, it truly shows.
Sunset's glow, a sight so divine,
Your baby eyes will surely shine.
Giant rock, stories untold,
A land of wonder, ages old.
Dreamtime tales, stars up high,
Baby, you're in for a wonder, oh my!

To Adelaide, baby, you're on your way,
Where kangaroos jump and koalas lay.
The beaches are golden, the skies so wide,
In this Aussie city, wonders won't hide.
Taste the fresh Tim Tams, hear the didgeridoo,
Adelaide's adventures await just for you.
With every new sight and sound to explore,
Baby, you'll cherish this land evermore!

In Perth, where the skies stretch so blue,
Kangaroos hop, and cockatoos coo.
Cottesloe Beach, with its golden expanse,
Invites tiny toes for a sunlit dance.
Fremantle's markets, alive and so spry,
Hold wonders and treats for a curious eye.
Swan River's shimmer, a sight so divine,
Reflecting the city's skyline in line.
Botanic gardens, where wildflowers bloom,
Perfume the air with nature's perfume.
Traveling baby, with wonder and glee,
Perth's beauty awaits for you to see!

In Broome's embrace, where oceans gleam,
Kimberley's beauty, a dreamer's dream.
Baby toes wiggle in sun-kissed sand,
Where boab trees in the distance stand.
Cable Beach waves, a lullaby song,
In this Aussie gem, you'll truly belong.
Red rock wonders, vast land to roam,
Tiny traveler, find your new home!

In Tasmania, where the wild winds blow,
Tiny traveler, there's so much to know!
Kangaroos hop, wallabies play,
Echidnas shuffle, keeping predators at bay.
Tall forests whisper tales of old,
Beaches shimmer, tales yet untold.
Baby's journey, under Aussie sun,
Tasmanian adventures have just begun!

In Byron Bay where the waves do play,
Traveling baby, you're on your way!
Lighthouse tall, beaches wide,
Golden sands where secrets hide.
Giggles rise with each splashy tide,
First-time wonders, eyes open wide.
Surfers dance, dolphins sway,
Oh, what fun awaits today!
Byron's charm, nature's song,
With each new sight, you'll belong.

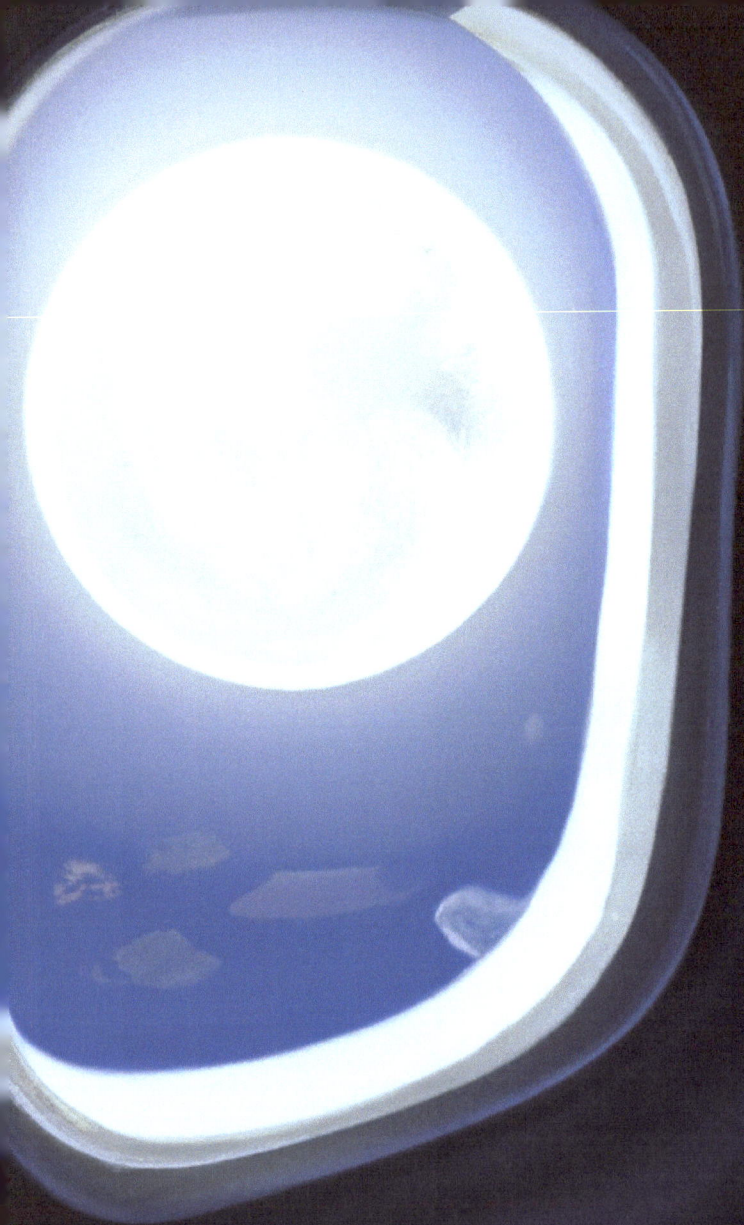

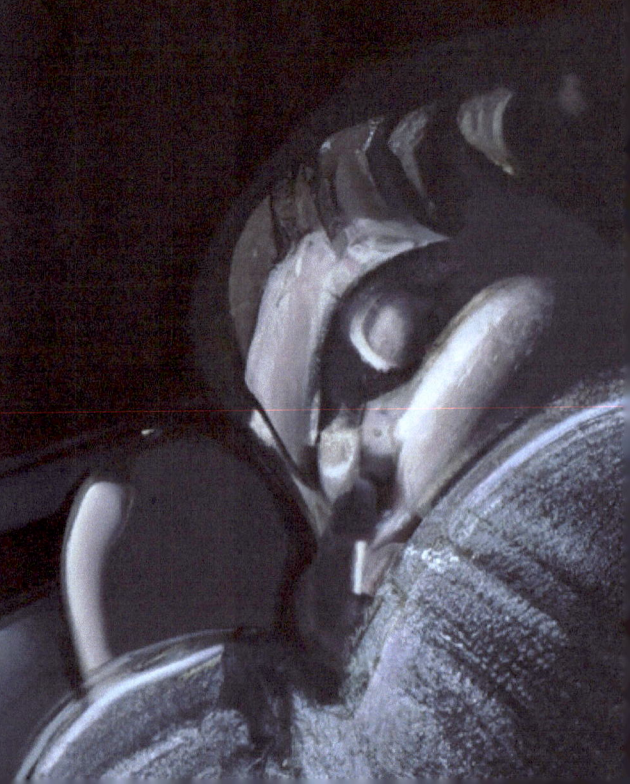

Journeyed 'cross the land Down Under wide,
From beaches sunny to desert's pride.
Tired but content, it's time to rest,
In your loving home, you're truly blessed.
Dream of kangaroos and oceans blue,
Australia's wonders forever with you.
So close your eyes, dear little one,
Your travel tales have just begun.

To Carli, my anchor and heart, whose love has been the steadfast light guiding me through every challenge and triumph. Your strength, grace, and unwavering support have been the bedrock upon which this work was built.

To Maverick and Myloh, my remarkable sons, you are both the pulse of my life and the joy in my days. Your laughter, inquisitiveness, and boundless spirits have filled our home with love and have fueled my imagination.

This book, a testament to perseverance and passion, is dedicated to you three – my most cherished treasures. Through its pages, may you always find a reflection of the love I hold for you.

About the Author

Rafiel Aharoni is a writer with a passion for kindling the flames of imagination and curiosity in children. He believes in the power of stories to inspire, teach, and transport young readers into worlds full of adventure and wonder.

While Rafiel currently spends his days studying towards dual degrees in Business Management and Cyber Security, he always finds time to create enchanting tales for his favorite audience: kids. He thrives on the balance between the calculated logic required for his academic pursuits and the wild creativity his writing allows him to express.

Rafiel's journey into the realm of children's literature isn't just driven by his love for storytelling, it's also fueled by his first-hand experiences spending time with children. He knows the value of a good story in lighting up a child's eyes and instilling in them a love for reading.

Although this may be Rafiel's first publication, it is certainly not his last. His work is characterized by a mix of whimsy, humor, and genuine understanding of a child's mind. Each tale he crafts aims to engage, entertain, and educate in equal measure.

When he isn't studying or spinning tales, Rafiel resides in the sunny city of Saint Petersburg, Florida. He believes the state's vibrant natural beauty and diverse culture are the perfect backdrop for dreaming up his next delightful tale.

Rafiel Aharoni: a wonderful father, a great husband, a dedicated student, a doting playmate, and above all, a devoted storyteller for children.

www.ingramcontent.com/pod-product-compliance
Lightning Source LLC
LaVergne TN
LVHW072132070426
835513LV00002B/79